WILD WORK

Who Counts the Penguins?

WORKING IN ANTARCTICA

Mary Meinking

Chicago, Illinois

www.heinemannraintree.com
Visit our website to find out more information about Heinemann-Raintree books.

To order:

Phone 888-454-2279
Visit www.heinemannraintree.com to browse our catalog and order online.

an imprint of Capstone Global Library, LLC
Chicago, Illinois

Edited by David Andrews, Nancy Dickmann, and Rebecca Rissman
Designed by Victoria Allen
Picture research by Liz Alexander
Leveled by Marla Conn, with Read-Ability.
Originated by Dot Gradations Ltd
Printed and bound in China by Leo Paper Products Ltd

15 14 13 12 11 10
10 9 8 7 6 5 4 3 2 1

Library of Congress Cataloging-in-Publication Data
Meinking, Mary.

Who counts the penguins? : working in Antarctica / Mary Meinking.

p. cm.—(Wild work)

Includes bibliographical references and index.

ISBN 978-1-4109-3855-8 (hc)—ISBN 978-1-4109-3864-0 (pb) 1. Earth scientists—Juvenile literature. 2. Scientists—Juvenile literature. 3. Antarctica—Research—Juvenile literature. I. Title. II. Title: Working in Antarctica.

QE21.C43 2011

508.98' 9—dc22 2009050396

Acknowledgements
The author and publisher are grateful to the following for permission to reproduce copyright material:

Alamy pp. **9** (© David Leatherdale), **25** (© Bubbles Photolibrary), **26** (© tbkmedia.de), **27** (© Dan Leeth); Bluegreenpictures.com P. **5** (© Ingo Arndt); British Antarctic Survey p. **24** (Pete Bucktrout); Corbis pp. **10** (© Image Plan), **12** (© Ann Hawthorne), **17** (© Johannes Kroemer), **23**; Getty Images pp. **4** (Cliff Leight/Aurora), **13** (Daisy Gilardini/The Image Bank), **15** (National Geographic), **18** (DreamPictures/ Photographer's Choice), **19** (Keren Su/The Image Bank), **22** (Ralph Lee Hopkins/National Geographic), **28** (Torsten Blackwood/AFP), **29** (Torsten Blackwood/AFP); Photolibrary p. **7** (Mark Hannaford/John Warburton-Lee Photography); Photoshot p. **11** (© NHPA); Science Photo Library pp. **14** (George Steinmetz), **16** (British Antarctic Survey), **20** (Karim Agabi/ Eurelios), **21** (Karim Agabi/ Eurelios); Shutterstock (© alysta) **background images**; U.S. Air Force photo/Tech. Sgt. Nick Przybyciel.

Cover photograph reproduced with permission of iStockphoto (© Mlenny Photography/Alexander Hafemann).

Some words are shown in bold, **like this**. You can find out what they mean by looking in the glossary.

Contents

Frozen Land

Welcome to Antarctica, the coldest place on Earth. Ice is everywhere. There's no sun in the winter. And you could get **frostbite** in the summer!

Thousands of people work here. **Scientists** are always learning new things in this frozen land.

The Big Chill

Antarctica is at the South Pole. It holds the record for the coldest **temperature** ever recorded: -128.6°F (- 89.2°C). The land is covered by ice that has been there for millions of years.

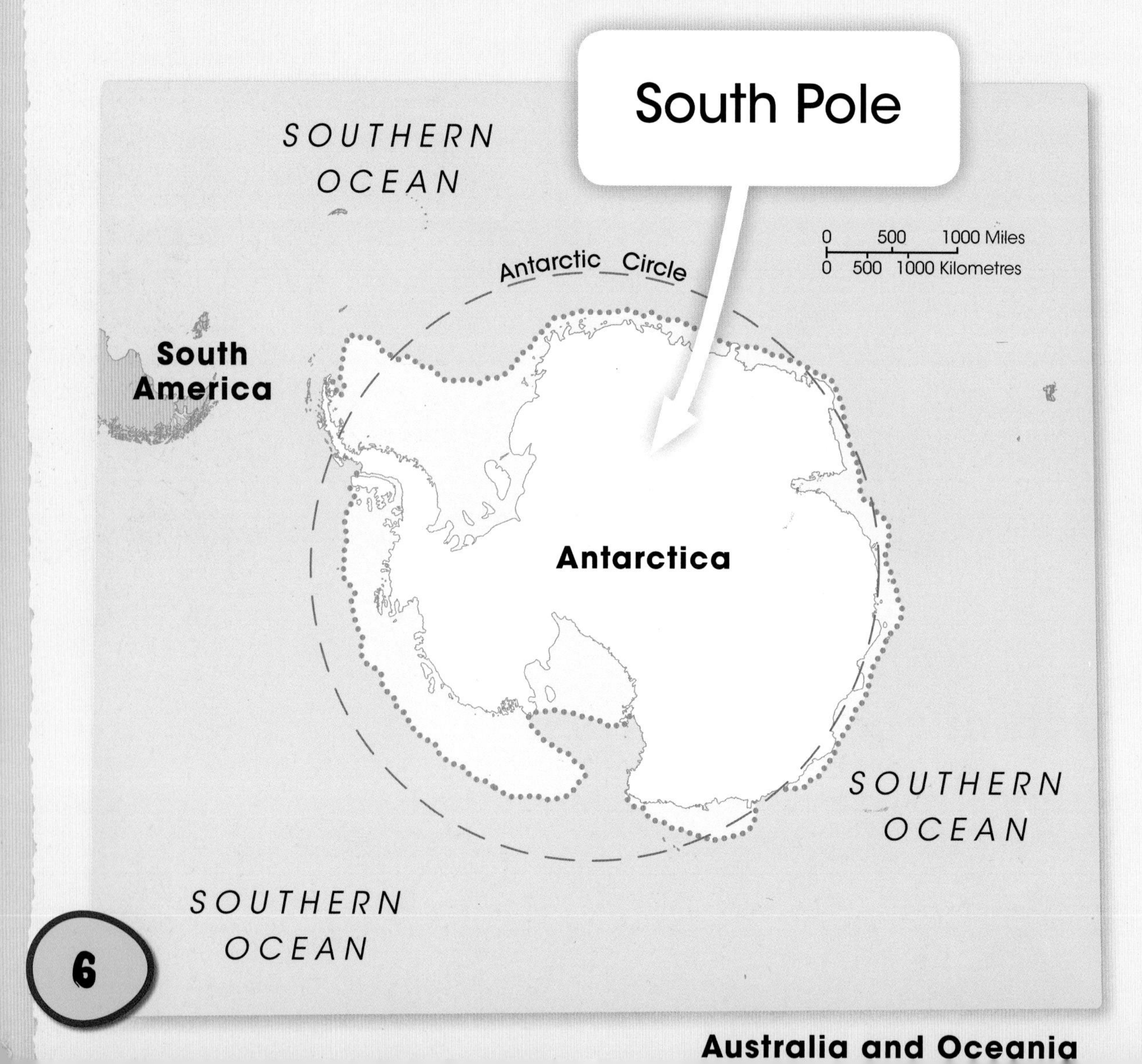

This is an Argentinean research base.

No country owns Antarctica. **Scientists** from around the world go there to study. The United States has three **research** bases there.

Prepare for Landing

There are two ways to get to Antarctica—by air or sea. Large planes and ships bring the big stuff, such as equipment and building materials.

Smaller planes bring the people and their gear. Most planes have skis to land on the ice.

Pilots in planes and **helicopters** fly **scientists** around Antarctica. They have to keep their engines running. They might not start again if they are turned off. Fuel turns as thick as syrup when it's that cold.

No one flies in the winter or when the weather is bad. Pilots can't land if they can't see the runway.

Smashing Through Ice

Big ships are needed to bring heavy things to Antarctica. The ships are built strong so they don't get damaged by the ice.

icebreaker ship

Some ships get there too early or leave too late. They get stuck in the ice. Icebreaker ships cut a path to free the trapped ship.

Drilling Through Time

Glaciologists (say *glay-see-ol-oh-gists*) study Antarctica's ice. When new snow falls it slowly packs the old snow into ice. Some of Antarctica's ice is 3 miles (about 5 km) thick!

The ice gives **scientists** clues about what happened in the world when it froze. Glaciologists drill out long pieces of ice. These pieces of ice can show ancient snow falls and when volcanoes erupted.

Glaciologists can tell what the **climate**, or average weather, was like 800,000 years ago. Computers compare today's climate to past climates.

Earth is getting warmer. Antarctica's ice is starting to melt. That cools the oceans. So everyone's weather is changing.

Counting Heads

Biologists study animals, such as penguins, that live in freezing Antarctica. **Scientists** see if there are more or less of them each year.

In late winter and early spring, biologists count penguins. At that time only the males are there guarding their eggs. The females are off feeding. The scientists know there are twice as many penguins as they can see.

Star Light, Star Bright

Astronomers say Antarctica is a perfect place to study stars. In the winter, Antarctica is one of the darkest places on Earth.

Even in summer, Antarctica is a great place for star gazing!

DID YOU KNOW?

A new **observatory** is being built in Antarctica. The star photos taken there will be better than any others taken from Earth.

Rock Hunters

Geologists search for **fossils** in Antarctica. The fossils show Antarctica was warm millions of years ago.

Antarctica is also the best place to find **meteorites**. These dark rocks from space are easy to spot against the white snow. **Scientists** have even found rocks from the Moon and Mars!

Help Me Doctor!

Everybody seems to do **research** in Antarctica. Some people even research the researchers! They study how Antarctica affects people in winter. This is a hard time. Not many people come and go. The sun is down all day long. People work, eat, and sleep differently.

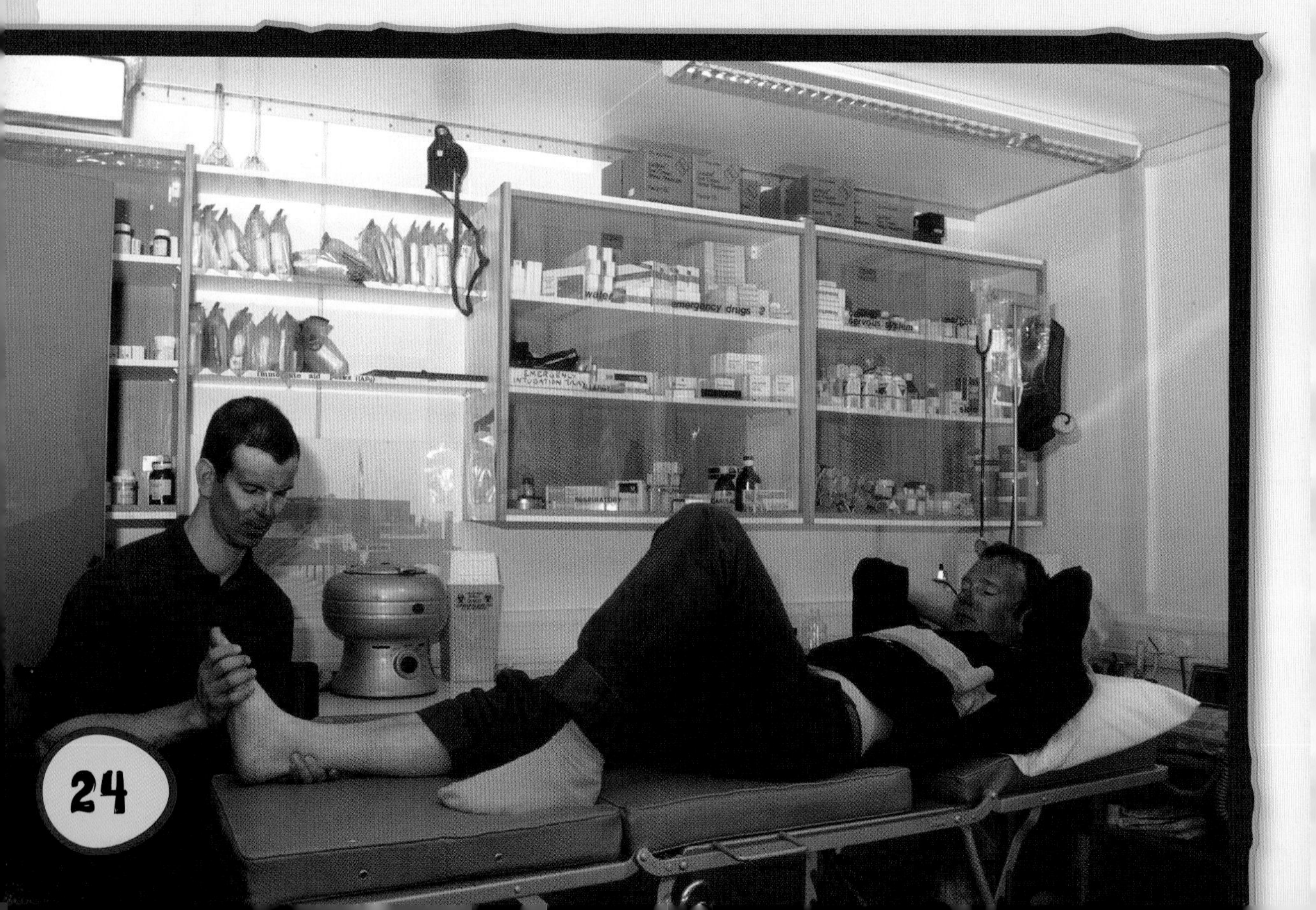

Sun lamps help workers feel better.

Helping Hands

Everyone in Antarctica has a job to do. Some people keep workers healthy. Others keep the bases running.

These postal workers make sure everyone gets their mail.

Some bases are like towns with stores and gyms. Other bases have only a few people.

Could You Work in Antarctica?

Many people want to work in Antarctica. Everyone must be healthy. They can't leave for emergencies.

Workers must love their jobs. They work 54 hours per week. Workers eat in cafeterias and don't have much space for themselves. But they say, "Once you work in Antarctica, you'll want to come back!"

Glossary

astronomer scientist who studies objects in the sky

biologist scientist who studies living things

climate the average weather for a place

fossil part of a living thing that has turned to stone

frostbite injury to skin after being frozen

geologist scientist who studies the Earth's surface, rocks and minerals

glaciologist scientist who studies snow and ice

helicopter aircraft that's able to hover and can fly in any direction

meteorite a stone that's fallen to Earth from space

observatory building used to study objects in the sky

pilot person who flies an aircraft

research to search for the facts

scientist an educated expert on one subject

temperature how hot or cold something is

Find Out More

Books to Read

Binns, Tristan Boyer. *Exploring Antarctica. (Exploring Continents series)*. Chicago: Heinemann-Raintree, 2007.

Osborne, Mary Pope and Boyce, Natalie Pope. *Penguins and Antarctica*. (*Magic Tree House Research Guides series).* New York City: Random House, 2008.

Sayre, April Pulley. *Hooray for Antarctica! (Our Amazing Continents series).* Brookfield, CT: Millbrook Press, 2003.

Web Sites

http://icestories.exploratorium.edu/dispatches/

Polar scientists talk about the work they're doing in Antarctica.

http://epa.gov/climatechange/kids/cc.html

Learn facts, play games, and find out what we can do to stop climate change.

Index